Code Black

Winter of Storm Surfing

Code Black

Winter of Storm Surfing

Tom Anderson

Published by Accent Press Ltd 2015

ISBN 9781783759194

Printed and bound in the UK

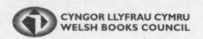
CYNGOR LLYFRAU CYMRU
WELSH BOOKS COUNCIL

Noddir gan
Lywodraeth Cymru
Sponsored by
Welsh Government

PART 1

End of January 2014

1

'Sand!' Ezra shouted. 'What's happened to all the sand?' He wished he'd paid more attention in Geography classes now – the teacher might have actually been on about something useful.

Today, the Porthcawl sand had gone. Vanished. Ezra was standing on rocks that nobody knew existed until a few days ago. He was staring at a reef, where once there had been a beach. Surfboard under arm, he was also looking out at some of the best waves he had ever seen in his life. The only problem was how to reach them.Ezra had surfed over sharp rocks since he was very young, but that was in places where the waves were *meant* to break over sharp rocks. Today he was facing not only the huge surf and the icy cold, but something else too. The thing that had taken the sand. The fastest current ever to flow past Porthcawl. If it could carry a billion tons of sand away to sea, then surely it could make light work of a skinny young surfer.

'Oh well,' Ezra said aloud. 'There's only one way to find out.'

And in he jumped.

2

Ezra was in trouble straight away. It was every bit as bad as it looked. The rip current was moving through the line-up – the place out to sea where surfers line up to catch their waves – so so fast even a boat probably couldn't keep pace with it.

He had walked to the furthest, sharpest, newest rock he could find and jumped out at the very top of the bay.

But it had been no use.

He had made it to within feet of where he needed to be to catch a wave, but that extra push was asking too much. The sweeping current got him and, without catching anything, he was moving quickly across the bay.

Maybe it can't be done, he thought. Maybe this rip *is* too strong. I've got to keep trying, though. It's worth it. It has to be!

And what an incentive there was to make it out there! These waves certainly were worth it! Rolling off the new shelf of rock, they were folding over themselves with a gorgeous anger, dark shadows of thick water. Each one was throwing out a heavy front lip, making an exploding cavern of water big enough for a surfer to stand right inside. Ezra knew that if he could just get himself on to one of those waves it would offer a long, long tube ride.

It didn't matter that his shoulders were burning, that the water was so cold it made his head ache. For now he had

3

to keep trying.

Looking back to land, he could see the Porthcawl streets behind the sea-front. They were sliding past as the rip carried him east. The land looked so silent, so safe, so… pointless.

He turned to head in before he got carried any further, and rode on his belly towards more of the newly-exposed reef. He knew what he was doing. He could get in safely, he hoped, and gently pushed on the tail of his board before he ran aground. His timing was just right. The whitewater drew back out to sea, and he climbed from the wet rocks to the dry ones with the footwork of an expert.

No joy at the first attempt. Time to try again then, and he began to run back towards the top of the bay.

3

Claire had made it into town early. It was a freezing cold morning when she left Cardiff, which told her that the wind had dropped. That was the one thing about these huge Atlantic storms that most people didn't mind. They brought in warmer sea air and prevented frosts.

So the cold being back could mean only one thing. The storm had passed.

Her gear had been out and waiting for days. Monopod, lens and cloth, can of air to clear sand away, a flask, thermals, warm coat, hat and gloves. Even though she hadn't been to the beach for ages, her stuff was always kept ready to go.

It was an easy drive down the motorway first thing in the morning. The heaters of her VW Trooper were on full, Wolfmother's 'Woman' was playing loud and her back felt fine. Mind you, she was lying down, but that was how she travelled everywhere. Claire would lie on a mattress in the back, while her husband Steve, the smiliest man in Welsh surfing, drove to wherever the couple needed to go. It worked too. Here they were, on their way to the Porthcawl surf, and Claire was comfy and content. As long as she could keep her fragile back warm this was going to be a good day.

Now they just needed to find where the surfers would be. There was a rumour all the sand had gone from

Porthcawl sea front, that it had left a surf spot like nothing ever seen before.

Thinking things through, she took a quick glance at a tide table, and leaned her head towards Steve up front.

'We need to get moving. How fast are we going?'

'Don't worry. We'll be there in no time.'

'Good. Tide's turning right now.'

And with that, Steve pushed the accelerator and gripped the wheel a little harder. Someone had probably paddled out already.

4

By the time Claire and Steve pulled up there were five surfers out. They all had black wetsuits, so she would have to wait for them to ride a wave to know who they were. She could identify most of the guys who were good enough to surf here, as soon as she saw their styles. Today though, that wasn't happening. They were out there, the waves looked great, but something was wrong.

She zipped up her thick, blue coat and stepped on to the sea wall. She waited five minutes, ten, fifteen, and still nobody was catching anything! It didn't make sense. Then there was the sand. Just like she'd heard – it *had* all vanished. How could that be?

These had to be the best local surfers. They wouldn't be out here even when the spot *did* have sand unless they were very, very experienced. So why weren't they catching anything?

Oh well, it was still a good idea to get a camera. She could always just take pictures of empty waves. The sound of the sliding door cut through the fresh winter air, as she peered inside the van. Ten frames per second. That ought to be about right. Should allow for a good shot of the whole line-up if no one rode anything. Empty waves made beautiful pictures anyway. They let you *imagine* the possibilities.

'You heading out?' she said to Steve, as she began

fitting the lenses together.

'Might as well,' came the reply, along with the usual smile.

'Great. Tell them I'm here and I want some pics. Maybe that will make them get on with it.'

'Sounds good. I'm motivated already,' said Steve, waxing up his board and handing her the key.

He headed to the jump-off spot, while Claire looked for a place to shoot. Then, as she headed towards the shoreline she noticed that one of the surfers was heading in. He was way over across the bay – must have just ridden a wave. *Nooo!* She'd missed it. And it was Ezra Hames too! He would have probably surfed it really well. She only hoped he wasn't done for the day, that he might head out again in a bit. She waved and he waved back.

Ezra climbed across the rocks further down towards the sea front. Once he got to the road, though, he didn't head inland towards where he lived. Instead, he began running back towards where Claire was, at the top of the bay.

'Nice of you to head over and say hi,' she laughed. He was probably looking to see if she'd managed to shoot his wave. She felt guilty. How could she best tell him she'd missed it?

'Hey, Claire.'

'I'm sorry, Ez, but I missed your wave then.' Better come out with it straight, she thought. 'I'm afraid, I was fetching some gear from the van just as you must have taken off. Looks like it was a good one though? You ended up *way* down the line.'

'Wave?' Ezra's face tightened, his forehead creasing. 'Wave! No chance of that. I got pulled down there by the rip.'

'By the *rip!*'

'I know, man. Brutal innit!'

In Claire's mind it all began to make sense. Now she saw why none of them had caught one. Oh, the cruelty of it! Mother Nature was such a tease. The best surf spot in Wales had sprung up, overnight, created by a storm so big it had made the earth shake. The *best surf spot in Wales* – except the waves couldn't be caught. Just Porthcawl's luck.

The best surf spot ever, and it had come with a current faster than most rivers.

The best surf spot – as long as you like the look of unridden waves.

'So you're running up this way to give it another go?' Claire asked.

Ezra's response was quick and certain: 'Too right! Gonna keep trying to paddle through that takeoff zone until either *it* stops breaking, or *I* stop floating. Whichever comes first!'

'Careful then, Ez. Look, another guy's just been pulled down the bay as well.' She wondered if it was Steve, then put the thought out of her mind. Steve knew how to look after himself. He would be careful.

But careful could wait.

Ezra knew it. Claire knew it. Everyone else knew it.

The best surf spot ever, and *someone* had to ride one before the day was out.

PART 2

New Year's Eve 2013:
The First Code Red Storm

5

The first really massive storm hit the British Isles around New Year's Eve. Back then, of course, nobody knew there would be six of them, or that they would pretty much come in a row.

That was why, back then when the first storm approached, the talk of a 'Code Red' swell had everyone so buzzing. There hadn't been one like it in a long, long time. That New Year's swell went red nearly straight away, and the best of the action was a place only twenty miles from Wales, but a three-hour drive over the Welsh border.

Hang on. Twenty miles from Wales but three hours' drive? Well, that's because of all that *water*. This is a place you have to drive around the sea to get to. It's a place that takes you over the Severn Bridge. It's a place that will take you up and down huge hills, through tiny farm lanes and across great cliff bluffs. And once you've done all that, you're basically looking back across the water at... Porthcawl!

Yes, Lynmouth is on the north coast of Devon, and yet everything looks and feels like South Wales. The water is just as brown, the rocks are the same type, the sky has the same wintery grey when a thumping storm is approaching.

And up until the end of 2013, it had always been the perfect place to head for a Code Red. Lynmouth was one

12

of the only places in the southern UK that could bend and hold a swell of that size. In huge storms, here was a place where the waves would still break with a shape that made them good to ride. That's why Welsh surfers sometimes had to spend hours driving only twenty miles away.

Code Red, by the way, is a surf term you don't hear a lot in Britain. It's rare for a good reason. It pretty much never happens.

Some of you may have heard of the horrible military drill when soldiers bully each other without the sergeant knowing. That is one use of the term Code Red, but in surfing the meaning is very different. In surfing, it means a swell has gone so big that when you look at it on the Navy's computer charts the centre has gone red.

Most charts that show you a swell and its size will use colours to highlight where the wave heights change. Generally they go from blue to about yellow. Dark blue is flat, lighter blue a swell about knee high. Porthcawl surfers might get excited at the sight of turquoise or light green – that's going to be head-high or overhead. Yellow or light orange? Well, that's a big swell. Dark orange? You're not in Europe any more.

And *red*?

Well, that's one of the biggest swells you'll ever see in the north Atlantic. A Code Red swell means cancel work. Call in sick. It means make sure you haven't got your kids with you. It means try to find a buyer for your Six Nations tickets, and cancel that holiday to somewhere else.

Since Code Red occurs almost never, when you do see one it's time to start planning. Working out where to meet it is an important decision.

A Code Red was exactly what was heading for South Wales and North Devon at the very end of 2013. As most of the non-surfing population prepared for their light-

13

hearted, fun-filled New Year parties, the keenest surfers were packing wetsuits, boards, wax, boots, gloves and hats into their cars and looking for somewhere to ride the swell. The first Code Red in years had popped up on the charts.

'Would you look at that *onion*!'

Three of the keenest Welsh surfers, Anne, James and Breige, were looking at Lynmouth on Google Maps, wondering what their chances would be of getting a bed anywhere near the place on New Year's Eve. The alternative would be Anne's old Fiat van sleeping all three of them.

'We've got to go there whatever happens,' Anne told the other two, looking up from the laptop. The other computer window she'd just opened had the raw data. It was indeed a huge swell. Red in the middle, like the rumours had promised, and that red centre was surrounded by rings and rings of dark oranges. 'Yeah. Hell of an onion.'

The storm's 'isobars' did look a bit like when you chop an onion in half. The lines were that tight. This number of rings normally meant hurricanes or superstorms. This could turn out to be quite a surf session.

'Look,' she shouted, in excitement. 'Butlins has a spare chalet going for a last-minute discount. That's only a little way down the road from the wave. Come on, guys. It's on. Let's do it.'

There was only one more thing to do before leaving. All three of them knew someone who would love to share this swell with them.

They placed a call to Claire.

6

'You know, people mostly judge you on one particular day,' says Claire, looking back at how she started surf photography. 'They'll make their mind up from what they see when they meet you. All that most people know of me is from down the beach, or out at the tip of a headland somewhere. Am I happy about that? Is that the "me" I want people to see? I'm not sure. One thing's for certain, though. They *don't* see that about three quarters of my day is spent lying down.'

In fact, Claire began that same New Year's Eve a long way from the stuff that had helped her to get her life on track again since that dreadful road accident. Her pain always came and went. It had *really* been getting to her that autumn, though, and in the early winter. To make things worse, her mother had fallen ill and needed constant care.

'The Lynmouth invite was both horrible and delightful at the same time,' she says. 'It came at a time when I needed to be reminded that the surf was out there. That there was this amazing thing I could do, to take my mind away from how difficult my life can be.'

She knew it was a great chance, but it was coming at the wrong time. For someone who found long distance travel so hard, and who was so badly needed at home, it was a step too far. Her mother wasn't sleeping. Her own medication was getting less effective too, and she had to decline.

'I said no,' she explains. 'But even though I missed out that time, it was probably still the moment when I realised I needed to start shooting again that winter. When I saw the swell onion go red, I thought I'd blown it. I thought that was it, and there was never going to be a swell that big again for years. I knew they were going to score some of the best waves they'd ever seen. But none of us had any idea that it was only the beginning, that there were five more storms like it to follow in ten weeks. The forecasts didn't really suggest it either. I don't think anybody had been given any warning of what was to follow.'

7

'It was a shame Claire couldn't make it,' James said to the girls as they hit the top of Porlock Hill, and Exmoor flattened out below. The South Wales coast had come back into view, and there before them was a new view of a place they knew so well. Porthcawl pier could be seen, sticking out into the ocean. To its left were the smoke stacks of Port Talbot steelworks, just as menacing when viewed from the cliffs of North Devon. The Vale of Glamorgan and Cardiff were spread out across the water, too.

For James, this surf trip was a shot in the dark. A snowboarder of semi-pro standard, he was fairly new to wave riding. James had surfed a lot when he was young, but never got really good at it. Then his life had taken him away from the coast. Now, with James recently turning thirty, his girlfriend Anne had dragged him back to the shoreline. 'Back to the source,' as James put it.

Anne and Breige, meanwhile, were experts of surf travel, not just in the UK but around the world. They had both seen a time when only a handful of girls surfed. Now though, they were relishing dragging a trembling lad along with them to seek out some heavy waves. Both had taught surfing at home and abroad. Both had done well in competitions. Both were now focussed on simply enjoying riding the best waves they could find – as often as life allowed.

Since her return to the surf scene nearly ten years before, Claire had become one of their best friends. Both Breige and Anne had been trying for a while to find a swell that might coax her out of the house.

James knew how special Claire was in their lives, too. He remembered well the first time he'd caught a bomb (an unusually large wave) back at Rest Bay, at the start of the summer. Sunlight warming the water had caused a thick fog. It was a murky day, and nobody else saw his ride. Then, just when he thought the wave was only going to exist in his memory, a figure appeared in the mist.

'This woman was holding a huge camera,' he remembers. 'She just said "Hi, I'm Claire. Would you like to see that wave again?"'

Yes, it was a pity she couldn't make it today, but it didn't matter. The three of them knew that memory was the most important way of storing your best rides. They also knew there would be more chances to persuade Claire to get out.

'It's winter,' said Anne. 'There's going to be plenty more swells.'

'Not like this,' said James.

'Hey, you never know,' Anne replied. 'Let's worry about today for now, eh?'

Lynmouth, of course, was firing.

James knew right away he was out of his depth. Their first view of the Code Red swell came as they drove over the top of Countisbury Hill. From there you could see for miles in all directions, including back over to Wales. Looking out to sea, Anne, Breige and James all saw that the horizon was stacked with lines. Rows and rows, wave upon wave. Each was a clear and crisp line of dark water, sliding smoothly through the brown ocean surface.

At the bottom of the gaping valley below, they could see the town of Lynmouth, with its fabled surf spot in full flow.

Bending around a kink in the coast, each line of energy was turning, slowing down and then peeling perfectly along the rocky shoreline and into the bay. There was a scattering of what looked like black dots on the water surface. Each time a section of breaking wave was going spare one of the dots would climb onto it. You could see a little white line in the middle of the wave where the dot was slashing and snapping across the smooth water face. Every single wave was being picked up by one of these surfers, and every single time the ride looked incredible.

For the three who'd just seen it for the first time from their car, this looked like the end of the rainbow. For James, though, this would be all about hiding his fear. *Facing* his fear even.

But first, he could give Breige and Anne a fright of his own. They'd asked him to drive since Bristol. The hill down to Lynmouth is one of the steepest in Europe, and going down steep slopes was something James *could* do. Okay, this time his snowboard had been replaced by his girlfriend's van, but that wouldn't stop him.

'James! My van! James! Slow down. James! You'll kill us all!'

'Thought you wanted to get there quick,' he grinned, as they carried on plunging towards the bottom of the valley, and the waves of their dreams.

8

Ezra, meanwhile, wasn't looking down anything as steep. Not in his dreams, or in real life. He had woken up to the sound of wind howling in the window and his phone pinging with party invites.

Without a car since starting uni, his best chance of a surf during the Code Red swell would be alongside the wall at Coney Beach. That was *behind* Porthcawl pier and harbour. The wind wouldn't get in there quite as badly, but even then, with this much swell about it would still be a battle against freezing, dark water.

Here it was, the swell that everyone had been talking about. But for Ezra, and most of the others who didn't have the time to travel anywhere, it was going to be a waste of time.

Mid-morning came, and he wrapped himself in a coat and hat before heading out on his bike. It was as he thought. Coney Beach was hardly offering classic conditions, so he took a ride along the Eastern Promenade towards the pier and the rest of the Porthcawl seafront.

In the howling winds it was becoming hard to look ahead. For a second he thought he might get knocked off his bike. *The storm is coming ashore early*, he realised.

And then he saw the spray from behind the pier for the first time.

It stopped him dead in his tracks. Ezra had seen waves

slap the pier and spray over the top thousands of times. He lived here. He'd grown up here. It was something you were used to. He remembered running the tide as a kid, dashing across the tarmac beach before the next wave came and drenched you.

This wave, though, was different. This wave broke *into* the pier. The spray coming over the top had a layer of dark water behind it.

Then another one hit. Boom! The ground shook. The waves were pouring *over* the pier – which meant they were... *bigger* than the pier.

Ezra began trying to work out just how big that must be, and then stopped counting. He dropped his head into the wind and pushed on. He had to see for himself what was going on the other side of that pier.

9

Across the sea and a huge drive away, the towering hills around Lynmouth were keeping all that wind out.

Breige, Anne and James knew as soon as they got into town that they'd found the right place to be. The normally sleepy village centre was crammed with cars and vans. Surf had transformed the place to a busy scene of soaking wet people running to and from the water. All along the pavements there were surfboards waiting while their owners quickly suited up. Clothes were getting thrown into rear seats. No time to do anything neatly. Not with waves like this on offer.

The three new arrivals were going through the routine just as quickly. James bullied his way into a tight parking space at further risk to Anne's van, while Breige peered out the passenger window. Another perfect wave was thundering past them, another surfer getting the ride of their life.

James had no time to be nervous. The girls were itching to get out there as soon as possible, and before he could think what he was doing there they all were, at the edge of the rocks, about to hop in. No chance of going back now, he thought.

One of the amazing things about Lynmouth is how easily you can reach the line-up. If you time jumping off the rocks right, a surfer can be out there and ready to catch a wave with hardly any paddling. Breige, Anne and James all arrived out back, behind the waves, together – and that was when James realised just how enormous the swell really was.

'A mountain doesn't move, you see,' he explained to friends in the days after. 'Unless there's an avalanche, of course. But that never *really* happens when you're out on the snow. That day at Lynmouth though... surfing... oh my God. It was like an avalanche going past you every twelve seconds.'

The girls were both on good waves quickly. James looked in from the channel as Anne reached the bottom of a wave easily twice her height. All he could think was how on earth he could get to the bottom of one of them in one piece. Once Breige had whizzed by, he was left alone, out at sea with hundreds of wave-hungry surfers around him.

Then he realised. If he was ever to stand on dry land again, he would need to *catch one of those things*. It was the only way to get ashore.

One of the worst feelings in surfing. No doubt about it.

To the other two, though, this was a moment never to be forgotten. The girls knew that the rest of the UK's surf spots would be struggling to deal with this gigantic swell. They also realised how rare such conditions actually were in this part of the world.

Here it was. Lynmouth, as good as it got. And what a ride. Speed and flow in abundance. Once you got down one, everything was easy. It was so much fun you would end up surfing your best almost by accident.

There would be days of it, too. All three knew to pace themselves. New Year's Day was forecast to be even better. A prediction that turned out a hundred per-cent accurate.

Overnight, for those who'd behaved themselves and

gone early to bed, the swell picked up even more. January the first, and what a Code Red it was!

'Best surf of the year so far,' Breige joked.

'Best surf of last year too,' Anne added.

'You got that right.'

At low tide, mid-morning on the first day of 2014, Lynmouth woke up to a mind-blowing display of perfect waves. They were breaking from the very top of the headland, right through to the start of the bay. Each ride of four hundred metres was simply a high-speed race against millions of tons of water, all draining off the rocks in front. There could not have been a better place to be a surfer on the planet.

Here it was. The swell they had all been waiting for.

One long ride would blend into the next, as the speed and rhythm of perfect Lynmouth made its way into their souls. A day where surfers could take their time thinking about what lines to draw. No need to change weight suddenly. At high speeds anything felt possible, and on waves like that, it usually was.

Breige and Anne had filled their wave-count the day before already. So, after getting another load of rides for themselves, they became focussed on trying to coach James into a good one. For him, the thickness and power of waves like this were taking longer to get used to.

'Get under them, James!' Anne kept shouting.

'I'm trying!' he yelled back. 'Every one I catch has smashed me!'

Battered but grinning, he fought on and on against a series of wipeouts. Each time he pushed over the ledge (the back wall of the wave), the energy would throw him forward and out. His ears were ringing. His shoulders and hips were yanked out of place. But by the end of the day he had caught one to take home, too.

'That's what you do with a swell like that, isn't it?' he said, shivering and pulling off his wetsuit as dusk fell. 'You *take the waves home* with you.'

As they drove, freezing and stiff, into the dark winter night, James was still full of this newest buzz. Rain was slowing them to twenty miles an hour in places.

'I've got the feeling!' he yelled. 'It's better than any mountain. It's kind of under your heartbeat, isn't it? It's amazing! Like as if I've got sea legs... only they're not sea legs. They're *wave* legs.'

'Surfing legs,' said Breige. 'Lynmouth legs. Some of those rides are probably as long as snowboarding anyway.'

'For sure,' said James. 'Except I feel like I've been run over by a truck. In a good way, of course.'

'Yeah. I'm ready to take the rest of January off from surfing now,' said Anne.

Fat chance of that, Mother Nature replied, under her breath.

10

Four days later, and there was already another Code Red brewing in the mid-Atlantic. By the end of the first week of January, it had hit. Twice in just over a week? The sea was making an *angry* start to the year.

In the hours before the storm arrived, the waves were firing. And this time, for just a few hours, it was clean and orderly enough for people to surf at home. South Wales came alive with line upon line of crisp swell.

The only problem? As those heading out at low tide soon found, the New Year's storm had taken away the sand!

There were big changes to the coastlines already, and surfers had only half a day to get used to the new shapes of their beloved breaks. By the following morning, Porthcawl pier was disappearing under exploding mountains of whitewater again. Giant waves and gale force winds from the second Code Red of the year had driven everyone indoors.

This time the fury was in a different league.

'We were lucky we didn't try to go to Lynmouth again,' Anne points out. 'Two days into the next swell the police and coastguard closed the line-up there. It was illegal to paddle out!'

And that was still nowhere near as big as the storms were going to get.

PART 3

Storm at Porthcawl
January 2014

11

An oceanic storm is one of the most powerful forces on this planet. Most volcanoes don't have the same destructive impact. Not even a nuclear blast can take up as much space. In fact, you probably have to go to Saturn or Jupiter before you find any moving object the size of sea storms on Planet Earth.

The influence of these storms is immense. Look at any world map. Every shape on there has been made by the sea, by wind and by waves. Britain is especially rugged. It's an island of inlets, nooks and crannies, each the result of what the sea and storms can do over millions of years.

But it doesn't always take that long.

In early 2014, lots of Britain's west coast changed shape within only a few weeks. That's how severe the storms were that hit in January, February and March. You would have had to be living on the moon not to have seen pictures on the news. No, in fact you might have even been able to see it *from* the moon, the weather systems were so drastic. Railway tracks collapsed into the ocean. Buses were picked up by surges. Cliffs fell into the sea. Coastal paths were destroyed. Aberystwyth nearly fell down altogether, while half of southern England disappeared under floods... Oh, and people rode waves, too.

At some points surfers must have been the only people

with anything to smile about.

And even they had to struggle from time to time. Ezra's New Year bike ride along the promenade was actually a pretty good taste of things to come.

Ahead of him, the pier was putting on a ferocious display. Waves were swallowing the whole thing, with water and foam flying hundreds of yards across into the town.

The short journey to the main road, and up to the seafront itself, took Ezra five times longer than usual. His legs were burning from fighting the wind. As he got close to where he would be able to see the ocean it became nearly impossible to keep pedalling. A woman in a thick raincoat was running sideways, nearly falling over in the wind and spray. Police were stopping cars from going up onto the seafront.

In the flying water and ocean mist, Ezra sneaked his bike past the barrier, and got off to push.

Five yards, four yards, three yards... Here came the ocean, and then... whack! The wind and spray hit him again with a new power.

Now he could see the full strength of the Code Red storm.

In front of him, stretching miles out to sea, were breaking white-caps thundering towards the shoreline. It was impossible to guess the size of the furthest waves, but they had to be bigger than his house. Trying to surf it would be like jumping into a giant blender. You would stand no chance. Taking a boat out would be barely possible – even a lifeboat. Now that was a scary thought.

Looking to his left now, Ezra could see the back of the pier. A hundred photographers, dressed like astronauts in all their rain gear, were pushing for the best position. They all wanted the same thing: to shoot one of the mammoth waves smashing against the stone and blasting high into the air.

'Ez! How you doing?'

Ezra turned round. Barely recognizable in his spaceman outfit was one of the local surf photographers, Tony John. 'Going surfing then or what?' Tony asked him.

'Er...' Before Ezra could say no, Tony was laughing.

'Don't blame you, mate. You'd get killed out there. A few of the crew were talking about surfing inside the wall later. Doesn't look very good though, eh?'

'Nah, just checked it,' said Ezra.

'I'm staying here anyway,' said Tony. 'Found a view nobody else has thought of. Gonna shoot the pier *and* all the people trying to get a picture. Looks amazing. Keep quiet, though. See you round. Happy New Year!'

'Yeah, Happy New Year to you, too.'

Ezra headed back into town, with the wind pushing him all the way. In seconds he had undone all that pedalling, and was back where he started. No last surf of 2013 for me, then, he thought. Oh well, hope 2014 gets off to a better start.

It would. And not just for Ezra.

Two weeks later, Tony John's photograph was on the fronts of newspapers across the world. It was an amazing shot. A gigantic wave walloping Porthcawl pier, while just in front a huge crowd of photographers aimed cameras skyward at the spray.

When Claire saw it, and read the name below, she sat bolt upright on her mattress back home.

'Tony!' she shouted aloud. 'Great! Wow! Steve, come and see this picture that Tony took. Amazing. To think that's the same day they invited me to Lynmouth.'

That was when she decided to get to the coast again soon. And that was what brought her to Porthcawl seafront a few weeks later, when she watched Ezra fight the current to no avail. It was only one short trip, in the middle of almost a whole winter stuck at home, but it planted a seed in her mind.

'I have as good memories of some surf sessions as the riders themselves,' Claire says, thinking back to that day in late January. 'That day when nobody could catch one! I thought we'd just seen the best surf of the winter. That's how I remembered it. The waves were so beautiful it didn't matter that most were empty. Only a few people actually rode one, all day. But the feeling I had that night, uploading pictures of the ocean... I thought it would never get any better.'

She insists that seeing Tony John's pier shots was the beginning of her whole adventure.

Because, looking back at it all now, every one of these moments counted. It all helped get her to the sixth and final storm months later. The surf day to end all surf days. The day the charts ran out of red, when all that remained was 'Code *Black*'.

12

It sounds great to be surfers when stuff like this is happening. But we should give some thought to what these massive storms actually *mean*. That's part of the deal you sign up to as a surfer. It's the agreement you make with Mother Nature. You have to respect the ocean and its ways.

'You have to remember it's never your friend,' says Ezra. 'That's not the role it wants to play in anyone's life. You might hear surfers say they feel as if the ocean is "part of them", but that's something you have to be very careful about. Because if the ocean ever decides to make you part of *it*, you'll quickly realise how small you are, and how very big it is.'

For a lot of people, those few months at the start of 2014 were hideous. For many, the most worrying part of it was how weather patterns we knew so well seemed to just disappear. The records broken and damages done were immense.

We had the wettest January ever. 'Widespread flooding and coastal damage' was how the Met Office put it. Did you know the huge storms in northern Europe came along with deadly cold weather in Canada and the USA? And, beyond that, Indonesia and some places in the Pacific grew unusually warm, with more rain too. It looks as though it was all linked in some way.

The cause of the whole thing? Well, we *think* it was a ridiculously fast wind that blows about ten miles above the earth, called the 'Jet Stream'. It is an amazing thing, and without it we'd all be in massive trouble. This huge wind, which blows above the part of the sky planes fly in, is basically caused by warm air from the equator. Heat makes air rise, and near the middle of the planet it goes so high above the earth that it gets heavy again and falls back down. Because the planet is spinning, the air doesn't fall straight, and gets spun across the Atlantic. That sends it up towards the North Pole. Underneath these long, straight winds are the low and high pressure systems which give us our weather. They are gently pushed along and kept under control. The Jet Stream means weather systems do what we expect them to.

At the start of 2014, when the weather people looked at a satellite, they were terrified by what they saw. The Jet Stream was running on overdrive, way faster than normal, and it was waving about all over the place. The result? Normally medium-sized winter storms were getting spun and whipped into these great giants, filled with wind and rain and all sorts of horrid events.

Porthcawl pier, built in the 1800s, held its own. But the cycle and skateboard tracks around the seafront, which had been built only a year or two before, lasted just one night once the big storms started. A loyal group of locals went down there to try to move the tons of pebbles and rocks back off them. The sea, watching and grinning, simply put it all back the next day. The same people tried the same repair job, which turned out to be pointless. A week later half the path was gone, ripped apart by flying rocks. What remained was washed away in days.

Stones seemed to be shifting everywhere else, too. At Ogmore-by-Sea, nearby, one surf spot almost vanished. A very important pebble bank, which local surfers relied on for a good quality wave, was gone one morning when someone turned up to surf it. At first, surfers assumed the pebbles had been spread across the South Wales shoreline. However, a week later a surfer driving up from Bridgend found the answer to the mystery:

'I know where the pebble bank is... It's half a mile *upstream*!'

He was right. An entire lump in the coastline had simply been lifted and carried a mile up the Ogmore river estuary. There it was, an entire spit of pebbles, exactly the same shape as it was when it had lived on the shoreline.

Meanwhile, most beaches seemed to have lost almost all their sand. A mystery which was never solved. Besides noticing it was worse at low-tide beaches (those you can only reach when the water is out), the sand loss was hard for even the experts to explain.

Out west, the rest of Wales's loose rocks were misbehaving, too. News crews love something that makes for a good picture, so 'Wales Today' were delighted to make their way to Newgale, near St Davids. On a summer's day the road there is beautiful. It hugs the seashore, giving you a lovely drive up the coast. By mid-January, though, the road had been buried in rocks, pushed up by the furious sea. When the local council came down to shift the mess and open the road again, the sea got even more angry. As if filling the road with rocks a second time wasn't enough, one freak wave then decided to give the TV reporters an even better emergency. A bus full of pensioners was lifted up and rolled into a field. Nobody was harmed (although a few ended up wet), but that didn't stop the news presenters from lapping up the drama. Wales loves its seas and its weather, and when the ocean and earth get mad around here, nothing gets people excited in quite the same way.

We will all live with the effects of these storms for years to come. In many places, the changes to Wales's edges will last for good. Of course, Aberystwyth's pagoda can be rebuilt, and Porthcawl's boardwalk. Changes in the actual *land*, though, cannot. Walk along Southerndown or Sker, Newgale or Newton, Llangennith or Llantwit and you'll see the results.

Every few hundred years the sea creeps inland a bit. But in 2014 it made almost a century of progress in three months. Everywhere you go, keep an eye out for the newly cut shapes of our shores. Fresh cliff faces, stacks of rock, lost edges of fields and golf courses. We've cleaned up what we can, but the warnings exist.

That sea has the power.

It will do what it wants.

All of Europe learned the lesson. It wasn't just the UK. Sand loss, falling cliffs, battering storms – France had it, Spain had it, Ireland got it so bad the whole country nearly washed away. Oh, and Portugal had it too. The last of the storms put Portugal right at centre stage – when Devon plumber Andrew Cotton caught a wave thought by many to be the biggest *ever ridden*!

Yes, *ever ridden*. And that's not Waimea, Jaws, Mavericks, Cortez Bank or Todos Santos. That's Europe. The Atlantic. Yes, the biggest wave ever ridden *on the planet* might have happened in the Atlantic. World gone mad, eh?

Just because of the Jet Stream being a bit naughty.

So, before we celebrate these storms as a surfer, it is indeed worth taking a minute to worry.

Because no one knows why it happened, or if it will happen again. It doesn't matter if the ocean goes crazy with hell storms every year, or if the next ten winters go back to normal. The events of early 2014 frightened weather forecasters *for life*, along with anyone whose job is to plan flood and coastal defences.

And, if as a surfer the whole thing hasn't scared you too, then watch out. Because the sea is nobody's friend. It may be beautiful, it may be mysterious, but in ten weeks that year, six storms told us that, above all, the sea is violent.

Sometimes, though, the highest forms of chaos can hold us in awe.

There are people out there who don't mind violence. Okay, not physical violence, or war. I'm talking about the violence that exists in a star blowing up, a shark thrashing its tail or a huge storm hitting a pier. There's a breed of people out there who are drawn to it.

With all that ocean power about, was it any wonder the country was full of surf tales? We can't change the damage the sea did, but we can definitely enjoy the beauty of what those storms allowed humans to do.

We know that a huge, final Code Black swell was where it all was ending. But it's important to remember what it was like for people chasing those earlier storms. They had *no idea* what was to come. For all they knew, each one might have been the last major swell of the winter.

All winter long, surfers were living right in the moment. They were surfing each session as it came, riding each wave as if it could be their best for years. Maybe even their best *ever*.

At the time everyone was convinced that the third Code Red was the best it would ever be.

That was another day when half the roads were closed, and even the most reliable big wave spots were supposed to be off limits.

But surfers are surfers, and someone will always find a way of getting out there. You can't bet on the size of the next storm, but you can always bet on a few fools trying to ride it. Yes, that sea may be violent, but in Wales there are always a few people stupid enough to enjoy the violence while it lasts.

PART 4

The End of January – Still Hunting the Waves

13

It was a Monday, which meant most of the surfers unlucky enough to have jobs couldn't get in the water at all. Unless they called in sick, of course. Or just quit work, full stop. It really was that good.

This was the storm (Code Red, of course) when surfers really got the chance to find out just how good the waves might be now all the sand was gone.

Ezra began the day with a nine a.m. lecture. He had to sit there taking notes on 'visual studies' knowing that three of his mates were waiting for him to get back so they could go on a surf trip.

The wind had south in it. A nightmare, most of the time.

Southerlies meant you couldn't go to many places in this part of Wales. But there was one important difference here. This swell was *huge*. Other surf spots, even ones facing north, were coming into play.

Ezra raced home to a car already packed. Leading the trip was Matthew Hapgood, owner of the shop 'Flow Surf and Skate'. He had closed up in a hurry, realising there was more to life than business on a day like this. The other two were Rob and George, surfers Ezra's age, both just back from gap-year travels in Australia. On their way through South Wales and out West, the idea was to begin at Tenby.

Tenby, I hear you ask? You'd be right to question it. There's never surf in Tenby, apart from in huge storms, when sometimes the place can deliver. Because of this, the boys had chosen it as their 'benchmark'. Once they knew what the surf was doing there, they could think about where else to go.

Now, it's important we realise how big a swell needs to be to get into Tenby. West-facing spots can have 'double-overhead' waves (this is a man's height) and Tenby will still be flat. To bend a wave around all the coastline between the open ocean and Tenby, you need a swell that... well, isn't really like anything on Earth. You need a storm the size of something you might find on Saturn or Jupiter. It happens once in a blue moon, and even then Tenby's swell usually fun-sized and a bit fickle.

Not this day.

'Hang on, are we in the right place?' Hapgood asked, as they pulled their car into view of the surf.

'Er, dunno. Never been here,' said Rob.

Their confusion was easy to understand. When they got there, Tenby's seas were too big to even consider paddling out. Waves were dumping and exploding the length of the beach. Meanwhile a thick, yellow foam was blowing up into the streets and carparks. Even in the heavy rain, there was salt water drifting through the air.

'Options then, boys?' demanded Hapgood. 'I didn't shut shop for the day to blow my chances of a decent surf. Where can we go?'

It was a mystery. iPhones and 3G could tell them that the wind planned to stay southerly, but it couldn't help them much more.

'Well, we go north,' said Rob. 'Ceredigion. We go north and we drive the coast. It's gonna be blowing offshore there.'

He had a point. With a swell this size, surf spots that nobody knew existed might lie besides the A487. The road hugged the coast almost the whole way up.

The quickest decision ever made on a surf trip sent the four back on their way. North it was. The stretch between Fishguard and Pwllheli was as close to uncharted as you could get for a surfer from South Wales. One or two legends said that waves broke in certain kinks in the coast, but in reality this was going to be old-school surf travel. An OS map, a tank of petrol and a shot in the dark.

14

'Road closed! You're having a laugh!'

The boys had forgotten about the rain. Wales wasn't used to massive swells and huge tides – the news cameras had shown us that. However, Rob had forgotten that inland parts were also struggling to cope with all this water. There had been a drought in the summer, and the ground was hard. A year's rain in a few weeks was the last thing Wales needed, and most of the small roads that cut north from Pembrokeshire were closed.

'We're gonna have to guess which ones are "closed" and which ones are *really* closed,' said Hapgood, pulling the OS map out again. 'Right, Ez, get on your phone. Find stories of trees falling. Oh, and check for landslides too. We need to avoid those for sure.'

'No signal,' said Ezra.

'Argh!'

'Alright then, it's a game of road roulette.'

The rain was the sea's fault too. The water might have felt cold, but in fact the oceans off Wales were almost three degrees warmer than usual. This was helping the storms find fuel, and it was why there was so much rain each time a swell came.

'No frost,' said Rob.

'You what?'

'No frost.'

'Yeah, we can tell that! It's about ten degrees.'

'No, I mean there hasn't been a frost *all winter*. Look. None of the trees have lost their leaves. The daffodils are up already.'

He was right. Four hours and twenty-three roads later, they arrived on the fabled A487, and the first thing they noticed was the colour green. It was everywhere. The hills, the bushes and brambles. Even walls of houses were going green with moss.

'Now we've just got to find a wave,' said Rob as they turned to track north along the coastal road. 'Oh, and we need to do it within an hour. Anyone noticed the time? It's gonna get dark soon!'

'Fine. Pick a lump in the coast and let's go look at it.'

'Alright then, that one.'

'That's a town! New Quay?'

'Thought that was in Cornwall.'

'No, there's a New Quay in Wales too. Ours is two words. New. Quay.'

'Well it's got to be a sign then.'

'Shut up! I *hate* Newquay.'

'What, Newquay Cornwall?'

'Yeah.'

'Well, give the name a second chance then. The Wales version can only be better, right?'

'Right. First turn off the coast road? Biggest town on the whole stretch?'

Of course they scored.

One of the rarest waves in the country. New Quay Point. Slabs of rock and the horrible smell of a fish-factory. A wave so hard to predict even the experts don't bother. And what did it look like for them that day?

'It was *pumping*,' says Ezra. 'There was one other surfer out there. Local boy. He was stokedto see someone else. Fully welcomed us, like. And the waves? Oh, the waves. Well, it was… what can I say? Don't want to sound like a kook exaggerating it… but it was… well, it was a three-hundred metre left-hand point break. With five people out. The cliffs were keeping the wind away too. What else d'you want to know? I can't say much else. That one guy in there? The local? He swore us to secrecy. Hang on, yeah… wait a minute! No! Let me take that back. It was crap in there. You hear me? *Crap*! There's no waves in mid-Wales. I was lying. All we did was drive around in the rain. Don't go there. I mean it.'

That was the day, they later realised, when one of the world's rarest and most spectacular big-wave surf spots had come to life. Two-hundred-and-fifty miles away, in Ireland, the mysterious 'slab' of Mullaghmore Head was attracting surfers from all over the world. Professional big-wave riders from Hawaii and the USA were tweeting photos of Air Lingus boarding passes. The bravest and best of the surf world were focussing on this same swell that had sent four close friends dashing all over Wales.

On the way home, Ezra wondered what the surf might have been like if only the winds had left the south alone… *If only.* Imagine what could have gone down!

Maybe the Atlantic was listening.

The next day, the wind dropped. Porthcawl was a low-tide show of terrifying barrels (waves curled over into tubes). The Flow Surf shop had to close a second day in a row, because it was time for Math, George, Rob and Ezra to go all over again.

15

Claire was going to have to give this one a miss, again. After her one photo trip to Porthcawl to see Ezra and to catch a wave, the pain had become too much again.

Long nights and short days were making life even tougher than usual. It was hard to get outdoors in the pouring rain and howling wind. Her mother couldn't leave the house, either. Steve was still going surfing, but would come back doing his best to hide a grin. If Claire couldn't go herself, he didn't want to keep reminding her how good it was. For her, watching and shooting *was* surfing, so she would be just as sad to miss out as anyone who could paddle out.

Of course, there was a time when Claire *could* paddle out, and the dark January days had also become a chance to think. With the curtains drawn, and in a silent house, the hours ticked by. Her mother slept, while Claire thought of the path her life had taken. It couldn't have been any different. She knew it, but still, it was hard to believe.

16

'Sports were my life,' Claire says, looking back to that time, long ago, when she could move freely without pain. 'Too much so, in fact, because when something like that gets taken away from you... Well, I'd lost my identity really.'

Claire still recalls the moment clearly. There she was, a twenty-nine year old. She was fit, healthy and seriously competitive about everything. Claire was an international basketballer and squash fanatic, a badminton and tennis player. She was a road cyclist (back when that sport was a lot rarer, and more hard-core), and of course she loved the ocean. That had come through Steve, who was a policeman at the time. His love of swimming had led him to be in the South Wales Constabulary Lifesaving Team. The galas and tournaments Steve competed in took the couple to the beach often, and Claire had plenty of chances to develop a big surf habit. Again, as with her cycling, Claire was one of a small handful of women in a sport dominated by men. She coped though, getting her waves and impressing the boys whenever she went.

So there she was, the best she would ever be. A twenty-nine-year-old sports fanatic riding a bike down a street one afternoon, pushing against the wind. All it took to change her life forever was one car.

Oddly, neither the driver nor Claire realised how bad

the accident was at first. The human body is no match for a machine, so the vehicle smashed her off the road. It brushed her aside like a hand might push a falling feather. There was the noise, the car trying to stop too late, the bike shaking as it smacked the pavement. There was the dizziness as she flipped over on to her back. There was the fear. *I must have done something bad to myself here.*

But there was no pain.

'I got up,' remembers Claire. 'Can you believe it? I got up, hobbled home and went to bed.'

No pain at first, anyway.

'Yeah, I got home and that was when my pelvis started hurting a bit.'

It was a slow, creeping pain. Claire's back began to freeze, one muscle, one bone at a time. She started feeling tired, too. Maybe she did need to go and see a doctor. It could wait, though. She just felt so... *sore.* Yeah, better lie down, she thought. She crawled upstairs, lifted her duvet and went to bed.

'And that's where I stayed, for years,' says Claire.

17

There was no time to sleep off their trip to New Quay. Ezra woke up the next day to the sound of moving water. He could literally *hear* the waves booming down his street. Ugh, he thought, the storm's still here. Then a look at the trees out the window showed him total stillness. Hang on. It was pumping again! It was time to clear the diary once more.

It's not too much of a challenge for a student to empty their day. A surf-shop owner can do it too, if he really has to. By ten on the morning after their road trip, Math, Rob, Ezra and George were all lining up to put on their leashes and paddle out towards everyone's favourite new wave: the low-tide barrel-fest caused by the missing sand.

In fact, Ezra had a theory that it was *extra* sand causing the waves to be like this. He thought that the whole coast had lost its sand apart from a little bank just behind Porthcawl seafront. Nobody could see it because it was beneath the surface. It seemed simple to him. Deeper water for the wave to travel through, then a sharp rise in the ocean floor causing the waves to tube.

Whatever the explanation, what greeted the surfers that morning was a new dawn of perfect surf.

'It was so heavy, people could hardly get down the waves,' explained Math in the pub later that night. 'It was as good as anywhere. No, it was better! France doesn't get that heavy and stay ride-able! Suggest anywhere... go on! It was *better*.'

Puerto Escondido, the Mexican Pipeline? Hawaii?

'Yep. It was better than those places, because these waves had such good shape. And also, there were only four of us out.'

What happened that day was that the normally horrid rip current decided to slow, for some reason. Nobody knows why, but it did. As a result, it also made the wave slow down too. This meant the thumping, racing tubes Ezra had already tried to surf several times that winter were suddenly completely user-friendly.

For a short while, anyway.

As soon as the tide turned things went *heavy*. Water was building up behind the waves, and there was a serious risk someone might break their board. Or worse.

But why did Math Hapgood think it better than anywhere *on earth* for an hour that day? It was the shape. On that one morning, at that one swell angle, with that day's wind, something extraordinary happened to the way waves broke. Maybe there was indeed a secret sand bar somewhere underneath it. We'll never know. The way waves were crossing each other suggested something very unusual about the sea bed.

Powerful lines of swell were breaking up and bouncing across the bay at odd angles. The result was big peaks of lumping water. The waves would then hit the shallow shoreline and lurch forward. The tubes were massive. Half of them would spit spray and air out of them as they pinched. It could have been anywhere on earth. Math was right. If it wasn't for...

'What about the cold?'

'Oh, who cares about that?' he laughed. 'When it's that good who gives a monkeys!'

18

January was passing into February. Valentine's Day was round the corner. As winter deepened, the evenings started getting a little lighter. Claire's mother was sleeping well, and Steve had been able to help too.

'Mum, I'm going to take you to the beach one day soon,' Claire whispered.

'Not before I take *you*, Claire,' said Steve. 'Your camera is coming out again this winter. It has to!'

'I know,' said Claire. 'We just need to find the day.'

Her medication was working better than over New Year, and two or three sunny days had flicked their light through the half-open curtains.

Thinking about the past was good in a way, but she needed to live in the moment too. Plus, she'd just seen the weather forecast on 'Wales Today'. Derek the Weatherman was predicting two or even three more storms in the next few weeks. The Atlantic was still going crazy. Each one was going to be bigger than the last, the Met Office feared.

The surfers, meanwhile, didn't fear. They *hoped*.

And so did Claire. She was starting to see that light.

19

'They told me to stop looking for answers,' she remembers. It had been twenty-one years after her accident, and nothing had worked.

'I'd had two back operations. Neither helped, so they told me to give up. To stop looking for a solution to the back pain.'

Claire winces at the thought of it. 'There was nothing that could be done, they reckoned. This was chronic back trouble and that was that.'

Claire has spent years coming to terms with that time in her life. Every hour she could be up and about, it probably led to four in bed. For anyone who hasn't had it, the effect of severe back pain is almost impossible to imagine. Your back is the part of you that holds everything together. It's known as 'the core'. It's what handles your body weight. It's what balances you as you walk. When the back isn't right, pain or numb feelings can pass up to the head or down to the legs with no warning. Nobody else understands, and some don't even believe in it.

It changed Claire's life beyond recognition. She could hardly remember what it felt like to go fast on a bike, to smash a tennis ball. They weren't even there for her to enjoy in memory.

And neither was the feeling of putting a surfboard on edge as you dropped into the bottom of a head-high wave.

She started to pine for all of these moments. That was when she realised there was one sport she missed more than all the others put together.

Then came 2004. A trip to the seaside and they happened to stroll past a local surfing contest in Porthcawl. After watching just two waves, Claire realised something. She was feeling pleasure! Okay, it wasn't *her* up and riding, but seeing the movements of a gifted surfer at one with a wave… well, she could enjoy that anyway.

The beginning of Claire's second love affair with the ocean had arrived. The key to it all would be a camera.

It worked immediately.

'I was given the gift of a lens,' she says, 'and that was it.'

This immediate force for good in their lives caught Steve up as well. Here was something he and Claire could do together, which would keep him active and healthy. And it was *fun*, too!

'Steve started surfing again, and of course I wanted to be part of it,' says Claire. Taking pictures was going to be her way of doing that.

Her first great shot was a buzz that matched anything she'd known in sport. The turn this guy'd laid down on a thick, warm-water wave was breathtaking. But the *picture* of it was her doing.

There it was in pixels on her laptop. She studied the look on the surfer's face, the intent, the focus on where he was turning. She could see how his legs were guiding the board through the smooth water, a deep scar of spray following the tail. There, just in sight, through thin, running seawater, were the fins of the board, holding the turn in place. They were harnessing the power that had come from the surfer's core. All of this had happened at speed, but Claire had it here frozen in a moment of calmness and beauty. Drops of spray hovered like a hologram above the top of the wave. Time was utterly still. A split-second explosion of power and performance was hers for ever. She knew the fine detail of this guy's turn better than he probably did.

But, Claire being Claire, she wanted to share. She wanted this moment to be *his* forever too. She wanted to let the rider see for himself what he'd managed to do on that wave, in that moment.

So next time she saw him on the beach she showed him.

'Did you know, I got a cracking photo of you last week!' Claire told the complete stranger. This was a leap into the dark for her. Surfers were too cool, she thought. She remembered how hard it was, being one of the only women on the scene all those years ago. She remembered how most surfers cared only about their own wave-count; how long it took to earn their respect.

But this guy's response was warm: 'Really? Can I see it?'

'Sure. What's your email address? I'll send it to you.'

She started to meet people straight away. After another of her early sessions, four-time Welsh champion Greg Owen approached her, to find out she'd taken an incredible picture of him doing an enormous, spray-chucking turn.

'It gave me pleasure to see the girls ripping as well,' says Claire. ('Ripping' means surfing really well.) 'There were so many more of them than when I used to go before. If I captured their waves on camera it was as if I was sharing in their session.'

This is a very humble way for her to see it. There may have been a *few* more female surfers than when Claire used to go all those years ago. Really, however, it was

Claire who helped get the numbers right up. Yes, ask anyone in the know and they'll tell you. Claire was one of the key figures in the boom of girl surfers in South Wales. She helped push that growth beyond anything it would have been otherwise.

It was Claire who put together trips out west for local girls interested in meeting each other, and getting better. It was Claire whose story inspired them to go when seas were big, and charge hard. It was Claire who shared her pictures of women ripping all over the web.

They bought her a custom wooden belly-board as a present, engraved with lines of poetry. It was a symbol of how special she had become.

Soon after that, more 'official' awards would follow. At the Porthcawl-based Welsh Coast Surf Club celebration night, she was presented with a special award called 'Spreading the Stoke'. They'd shortlisted her for 'Surfer of the Year' too, and she narrowly lost to someone who had just won a European and British title in one season.

She became a hero to many people: male, female, young, old; top surfers; Welsh legends. Ask them who they admired most in surfing and many would say ...

'Who's that lady with the smile? Beach Spirit? That's what she goes by on the internet... *Claire*, yeah, that's her! Claire Beach. She's *such* a hero. She's got more stoke than *anyone*.'

She became an expert, too. Claire could predict swell as accurately as the best of them. She could predict the winner of a contest, the outcome of a close heat. She could tell you who was ripping and who was riding the wrong board that season. It was no wonder she was getting calls from everyone whenever the surf looked good.

And as for that winter of 2014? The season of epic storms? Well, surfers in South Wales have a theory about those storms, too. Right or wrong, the theory sounds good. It sounds like something you *want* to be true.

What if the ocean's game was really all about Claire? What if, as they say, the sea knew she was down on her luck again? What if the sea was trying to coax her out?

It has to be true. That's the real explanation. The New Year's Code Red storm was for Claire. It was to try to draw her back to the ocean, back to the source. When she couldn't go, the sea gathered its strength and tried again.

And again.

And again.

And… again.

Four storms, all red in the centre. Claire wasn't hearing the call, and *that's* why Mother Nature kept them coming.

A fifth swell. Deepest shade of red available on the Navy's swell charts. Thirty-five feet in the eye of the storm, the centre of the fury. A *big* swell. Claire nearly made it out. She was nearly ready.

'Not quite,' she told Steve, though. 'I want to choose just the right day. But it is going to happen. Soon. I can feel it.'

'Okay,' said Steve, smiling patient, confident.

March arrived. Winter had to back off soon. Surely the chance was running out. But Steve could tell when Claire was right.

'Anyway, I want to shoot the reef breaks,' she told him.

Yep, thought Steve. She knows something. When Claire was this determined, she had to be listened to. It was that simple. But did she know what was around the corner? Did she really know we were on the brink of the swell to end all swells?

Something was building on the ocean charts.

'The Esplanade and the Porthcawl Point, Steve. They're my favourite places to shoot, because of the danger there.' Claire knew what she was looking for. 'They say there's no sand behind the Point either. It's got a deep-water channel now. Apparently it can hold waves of any size.'

'That's true,' Steve confirmed. 'You know about it even when you haven't been there!'

'Yes,' said Claire. 'And that's where I want to head. The danger is the important bit. Danger attracts the best quality surfers.'

And then they ran out of colours.

'Steve. Look! Look at the centre of that *onion*.'

Steve peered at the laptop and his jaw dropped. Must be a mistake with the graphics, he thought. Surely that was meant to be another dark red? Thirty or forty foot, like the others. But then he saw the rings around the outer edge of the dark centre, four-hundred miles away from the eye of the storm. *They* were dark red and purple. That meant the centre had to be even bigger.

No. Claire and Steve weren't seeing things. The Navy charts had run out of colours to code the wave sizes. Code Red was a thing of the past. This onion had nothing but *black* at its core. A big black splodge where the storm had gone off the scale. An event horizon. This, was a Code Black. The first of its kind in modern forecasting.

Claire was calm, but you could feel her excitement from Cardiff to Porthcawl and further. It must have been carried on the light offshore winds.

'This is it, Steve! It's the one we've all been waiting for.'

PART 5

Code Black

20

Ianto had been keeping an eye on the sea at Porthcawl's headland, the Point since just after low tide. He began most swell days driving down to check it. Usually he would then do a few hours' work, setting his watch to the right stage of the tide and not worry about it again until it was time to surf.

However, one morning in late March his routine was very different.

'I didn't want to miss it starting,' he remembers. Ianto was a plasterer, much in demand. He had a big job on, but today *nothing* could be more important than the waves.

Unlike most of the epic surf sessions in the winter so far, this one wasn't taking anyone by surprise. This was no tiny window of calm between winds, no shifting tide or sudden rise in swell size. This was a perfect day on every possible chart, predicted accurately, from days before.

The sun was warm for March. There was no wind at all, and conditions couldn't have been better in any way.

Still, Ianto wasn't leaving anything to chance. The minute the seas started to break, he had to be in there. No. He had to be in there even *before* that. It was his duty.

With the sand shifting around, the Point hadn't been sticking to its usual tide timetable anyway. Seas had been breaking lower on the tide than any time in its history. All winter long, people had been getting barrelled. Ianto had surfed the Point for thirty-five years. He'd worked his way to the top of the chain there, one of the most respected locals at one of Wales's best waves. Lately this spot had waves as good as anyone could remember. And today? Well, it felt like a grand finale. It was the Point's last hurrah before summer.

Looking towards the west, he saw a wave pound Porthcawl pier for the millionth time that season. Its spray drifted gently through the windless air. There was something so much more *ordered* about these waves, he thought. Normally the explosions off the pier were followed by a lump of broken water walloping off the end. This time, all that came into the bay was a thick line of energy. A deep, dark groove in the surface of the ocean, bending its way into the bay.

Behind it was another one. Then another, and another.

Ianto watched the pulse cross Coney Beach, and take shape at the Point. It darkened even more, and began rising out of the water. As the first wave began to pitch a glint of sunlight shimmered across its face. Then the wave pitched and broke, hollow and heavy, all the way across the Point and into Trecco Bay to the east. The folding tube was followed by a thundering lump of whitewater.

Each of the next waves in the set did exactly the same. Ianto could hardly believe what he was seeing. He looked at his watch. Mid-tide. It was starting *already*?

There were three other people watching it this early, too. He didn't know who they were or when they were going to paddle out. It wasn't quite time, but the presence of others meant he needed to put his wetsuit on. Ianto had never seen it like this, and he knew it might never happen again. Today was a surfing day. It was *the* surfing day, and now he had to get on with it.

21

Ezra woke up at nine-ish that morning. There was no hurry. He knew high tide was when it would all *really* go down. He quickly put together his usual breakfast of Marmite on toast and a cup of coffee.

It was midweek and he had no lectures. Things couldn't have fallen into place better. The weekend was fading into memory, which was exactly what he needed. His last surf had been on Saturday, in a competition on the Gower. The Welsh Inter Clubs. Ezra had done terribly.

'Yeah, the Inter Clubs, man,' he groans, looking back. 'I blew it as usual. Just like every comp.'

Nobody doubted that Ezra was one of the hottest surfers in town. He had been for years. But wearing a contest jersey was, for him, a wave-riding equivalent of putting kryptonite round his neck. He hated competing, but had gone to this one out of loyalty to the Welsh Coast Surf Club.

It was the usual routine – designed, Ezra felt, to make quite sure he would surf his worst. He had to wait all day for a late-afternoon heat. When his turn did come, it was in the tricky Langland reef break known as 'Crab Island'. He was against a couple of locals, in horrible, tiny, windy, conditions. All he could think about was the pressure.

'Ugh, yeah, the pressure,' he groans. 'Contests are always like that. There was plenty of time to prepare and over-think. The team wasn't doing great and they really needed me to surf well. That kind of situation doesn't do me any good. I get in the wrong mindset, like? And then I throw it, you know what I mean?'

Welsh Coast's team manager and captain, Greg Owen, told Ezra exactly what he thought of him. Top sportspeople often do that. Ezra was given a detailed breakdown of how and why he'd messed up his chances, before getting a lift home with two other team-mates who had lost their heats too.

'I wasn't in the mood to surf for a few days after that,' Ezra recalls. 'I remember driving home, the three of us, sulking. I remember looking around and thinking… Well, it was true… Van full of losers, like!'

A Saturday evening of junk food, and the feeling you don't want to surf ever again. That was what Ezra was doing when he got a text from George:

Check chart for middle of the week. Code BLACK this time!!!

Suddenly, he *did* want to surf again. In a few days, of course. Could there be a better way of getting over a contest loss?

Ezra actually surfed somewhere else, just after breakfast, when the day came. 'I had to,' he remembers. 'It was only gonna be that good for one day, so I needed to get as much in as possible.'

His choice of earlier session? The sand-less seafront, again, where he had gradually been getting better at playing the rip.

'It was great there, too, of course. But I wanted to save my arms. Paddling that rip was hard, and all I was thinking was how good the Point was gonna be that afternoon.'

The session had gone quite well. Things were simple enough so far. The swell was big, and there was a lot of water moving, but nothing really scary. Then, on his last wave, there came a sudden feeling things had begun to change.

Having already decided this would be his last wave, Ezra stroked into it carefully, without worry. He got down the wave and turned towards the face. The lip (tip of a breaking wave) was somewhere out ahead of him, and he began looking for a chance to head up the wave. But suddenly it felt as if the whole patch of water he was on had slipped on to a different track. The wave's bottom was drawing him down the face, yet from somewhere he had speed. Ahead of him he could see the curl starting to pitch and quickly dropped his head under it. The sound of open air suddenly became an echoing, whooshing noise, and ahead of him was a dark tunnel of water. He peered toward the exit, and then got a load of water in his eyes. Holding on, he aimed for the beach and next thing he knew he was standing clean on his board, in the whitewater. He had made it out of a *really* tight tube. That was amazing! This was epic! This was happening at *the end of his street?*

Straight away he could feel himself swelling with satisfaction. He deserved that wave. He had been working really hard all winter on his 'pig dog' technique. This was a technique that enabled a surfer to ride a tube, when their stance wasn't allowing them to face the wave. An American had given him some tips during a trip to Bali in his gap year.

'I had an idea of what to do,' Ezra says. 'But it wasn't really until that winter that I got any practice. That

American guy said it was all about dropping the shoulder down. He said it as if he thought I could just try it out a million times once I got home. I told him, you know, that we live in *Wales*. He hadn't realised how crap the surf is here most of the time. We never get to tube ride at home! Well, apart from that winter.'

His first session had been a success, but for Ezra, great waves were now the norm. He needed more. This was the day of days. This was the Code Black. This day needed to be approached as if it would never happen again.

'That barrel I had in the morning,' he recalls. 'It was little. I just got my head washed in it really. That other one, though… the one I had in the afternoon? Now *that* wave…'

Yes, there was more to come for Ezra in this swell.

A *lot* more. Like Ianto, and like hundreds of other Welsh surfers that day, he had a destiny to chase.

22

'Forget about the surfer in you for a second, Steve,' said Claire. 'Think as a *photographer*. We need to go where the pictures will happen. Think carefully. We need to work it out, to get it right. Where's the best show going to be? You'll get your surf, but *I'm* shooting the Point.'

Back up the M4 in Cardiff, the chase was almost on. Claire had been watching the storm turn Code Black as closely as anyone. The other surfers' excitement had been felt by her and Steve too, ten times over.

'I want just one day when it's gonna be worth my while,' Claire had said earlier that winter. As soon as this last storm of the season popped up on the charts, she knew that *this* was the swell to provide her with that day.

Steve thought the storm would follow its waves to shore, like the others had done. He expected Wales to get another pounding. But Claire had kept faith all along. She told Steve right away: '*This* storm is staying out to sea where it belongs. There's going to be a huge swell from it, and it's going to be met by no wind and sunny weather.'

And here it was. No wind, sunny weather, huge swell.

Claire's swell. It had to be.

As usual, Claire was lying in the rear of the van, staring up at the ceiling as Steve drove. This time, though, she kept sitting up from time to time. Surely getting to Porthcawl didn't take this long?

'Come on, Steve, can't you drive any faster?'

She could feel the van rocking through familiar turns in the journey. They'd slowed down off the motorway. She was sure of that. They'd also made it through the main roundabout. Next, she felt the speed bumps of New Road, then the change in weight as the van swung up the cracked track to the Point. Nearly there!

Steve's cry of delight was the first warning.

'WOOOOAH! It's amazing out there!' he yelled.

The side door of the van slid open, and out went Claire into the warming spring air. A set of liquid gold waves poured straight down the Point, as if they had been waiting for her to arrive. She counted off the waves. One, two, three, four, five...

And on it went. An *eight*-wave set? Each one of them was well overhead, and lined up perfectly. Several of them had gone unridden too. Where were all the locals?

'Ianto was out there first,' she recalled later. 'Ianto Bowen. Everyone knows he's one of the top Point surfers. He really knows the place well and can ride it big, so that was all I needed to hurry on down the rocks. I just thought *here we go*. These people are going to put a show on for me now.'

Steve was stuck between his urgent desire to get in the water, and his fears for Claire's safety. She had thrown the pop-up stool she normally used straight back in the van, and was looking for a spot to set herself up on the Point itself.

'Claire, those rocks are really hard to walk over,' Steve pleaded. 'Come on, you've fallen over before...'

'I'm fine, Steve. Just enjoy it. Go on, get in there. I'm going to be okay. I promise I'll watch out.'

Yes, Claire had tripped over rocks in the past, twice. Strangely enough, she was fine both times. She thought it

67

was because her medication relaxed her back while walking. But Steve thought it was just chance, and didn't want to try for third time lucky.

But then there was the surf… Steve watched another set of waves detonate at the top of the Point and peel into the bay.

'Okay, Claire,' he said. 'Let's do what you say.'

And in he went.

Claire was glad he'd gone. So what if she had fallen over before? Life is about risk sometimes, and this was a no-brainer. She had to get on to the rocks. That was where the view would be best. It would be worth it. Today she could see some of the best rides in her life, and the light… oh, the light! It was like a studio down there. Sun was shining right into the hollow waves. Everything was full of colour.

Her feet took a careful grip of the first rock. She could see her spot, twenty yards ahead. She would be careful. She would get there fine.

It took about ten minutes, which was long enough for Steve to make it out back and two more sets to pour through. Once Claire got there, she dropped her camera stand to the ground, trained her lens on the line-up and took a deep breath.

'Okay then,' she said aloud to herself. 'Let the show begin.'

23

Ever thought what it might be like in the centre of a storm that size?

It must be incredible, insane, impossible – the sea throwing fifty-foot waves around like you might swish water in a sink. The winds would be enough to lift a helicopter. This would be the kind of storm that could snap an ocean liner in half.

So how can something as straight as a wave come out of all that chaos? Well, it's all about distance. These storms are so big that whole countries could get swallowed up in the middle of them. The eye of a storm like this is being moved by Planet Earth itself. That's what drives it, like a big system of cogs. Earth is the main cog, the Jet Stream like the fan belt. Powered by the sun, the storm is a turbine, or a piston in an engine that can run for weeks.

And what comes out of it? Well, as you move away from the anger in the centre, all those fifty-foot lumps of water start to join each other, and smooth out. They form lines of energy which begin to run away from the storm and towards land. The lines order themselves into rows as they accelerate through deep, deep ocean.

Sometimes the lines catch up with each other . Boats out to sea have seen it. Bigger waves chase smaller ones down, and eat them. They consume them. They *assume* them.

That's how we get 'sets' when a swell has travelled a long way. Waves start to join and form bigger, more powerful mega waves.

Every now and then, when a storm and a swell are truly massive, the mega-waves can even suck *each other* up, too. That's normally towards the back of the swell. It's as if the waves are all going into battle, and the biggest, most powerful get to stay at the back. The ones in charge.

All the way through a storm, the ocean will push these waves out and send them racing for land.

But every now and then, the storm might clear its throat in one big heave, and send one super-wave chasing after the pack. A wave that will make the rest of the swell seem like no big deal at all.

It must have been days before, when the ocean made up its mind. *That* wave had been on its way already. It was there, silently marching through the sea as Ezra drove home in his 'van full of losers'. It was probably half way here when he looked at his timetable on the Monday and saw no lectures later in the week. *That* wave would have been starting to feel the bottom of the Welsh sea-bed as he was waxing up his board and heading to meet Ianto at the Point.

Perhaps *that* wave had known all along what to do when it got there.

The question was, would Ezra?

24

'Well *I* reckon it was the biggest wave out there that day,' says Ezra, sitting in his back-garden, basking in hot summer sunshine and looking at a print of the picture. 'As soon as it started to feather I wanted it. Once the others saw me paddle they knew it was mine. I was going, and that was that.'

He holds the image up, to avoid the sunlight reflecting off his iPad. Then he stares in silence and you can see the memories running through his head.

'D'you know, it's hard to imagine waves like that breaking on the Point now, eh? Middle of the summer and all... I miss it, you know. Looking at this, looking *back* at it. Well, it makes us realise how lucky we are in Wales to have winters like we do. I don't really mind the cold, eh? I know it's easy to say when we're surfing in shorts and it's boiling hot, but I mean it. I do. It keeps the line-ups quiet.'

He stares again, right at the centre of the image in front of him. He stares so hard the frozen wave almost begins to move again.

'Think about it,' he says. 'Think about Australia, France, California. You'd surf waves like that with *millions* of people if you lived in one of those places. But here? Wales? Well, that day...'

He rolls his eyes upwards in his head, like people do when they're trying really hard to remember.

71

'Yeah, that day… well, there was only a few of us out. I'm still finding it hard to believe it really happened like it did.'

25

'It was the day I had been looking for,' says Claire. 'And there were so many people out. Well, for the Point, anyway. I know if you had surf like that in Australia or California it would be heaving with people. But for the Point I'd say it was a fair old crowd.'

Ianto had it to himself for only ten minutes, before others made their way in too. Three-times Welsh champ Greg Owen arrived in the line-up not long after that, followed by a crew of dedicated surfers who would all excel in these hollow, dangerous conditions. There was local tube-specialist Rob Miles, Welsh team member Amy Murphy as well as top Porthcawl chargers George Schofield and Chris Seage. That was along with about fifteen others who didn't care for names, contest records or sponsors as long as they got the wave of their dreams in the next few hours.

'It was the best surfing I've ever seen outside competition,' says Claire, remembering the standard in the water that day. From where she had set up on the rocks, she could see everything that was going on. She had a clear view of the deadly first section as it broke over shallow, sharp rocks. That was her priority. However, Claire could also see across into Coney Beach, which was also about as good as it could get.

'In the breaks between sets on the Point, I kept turning

my camera over there too,' she says. 'Coney was better than I've ever seen any beach break in Wales. Each time a set hit the pier I would line up my lens and wait. I could shoot a wave with unknown riders on it, all the way across Coney. Then it would arrive at the Point and someone at the very top of their game would catch the wave for me. That's what it felt like. It was as if these incredible surfers were giving *me* my own private display of their abilities.'

It was while training her camera towards Coney that she noticed Ezra arriving. He had chosen to paddle out from the beach and head around the back of the Point. It's a plan that takes a bit of faith. As you do it, the waves always look as if they're about to smash you onto the rocks. The water there is deep, so that rarely happens, but today Ezra looked *tiny*. He was completely at the mercy of the swell as he just squeaked through an enormous set.

'He kept so calm,' Claire remembers. 'He didn't seem in any hurry. He took his time, worked his way slowly into the session.'

That wasn't quite what was going on in Ezra's mind, though. He wanted to appear cool and relaxed, but inside he was full of adrenaline.

The set that came through as he paddled out was the most powerful he had ever felt in Wales. He had to use every ounce of energy in his arms to avoid being washed over the rocks. After that he took a longer, deeper route behind the Point. He didn't want to take *any* risk. The surf was too good to miss because of a silly injury paddling out.

His first wave was smaller, and he focussed on doing a few turns through the lip. It was long, though, and he noticed straight away the amazing range of moves that could be done that day. Cutbacks, top turns, floaters. He caught a few more waves and was trying to get his fins out as high as he could. It wasn't long before he fell on a few, but that was fine. The water was still freezing cold, but without wind the day felt mellow.

All was going to plan. He was having a good session. Normally the rising tide would make the waves a little gentler, a bit less shallow. Today though, that wasn't happening. The fun-zone was shrinking by the minute, and the waves were growing hollower.

Paddling back out after a particularly heavy one, Ezra saw Rob Miles drop into a tube that seemed to drain water off the reef as it went by. He saw Rob's face inside the wave. Ezra must have been only feet away. He could see Rob's eyes, and wondered what they could see looking back.

Ezra had to get one like that. He just had to.

He remembers making the decision: 'Yeah, I saw Rob get one and it looked amazing. So I thought, that's it. I just went for the barrel after that!'

It was difficult. At the top of the Point an extremely competitive situation had developed. With all sorts of champions and sponsored riders out, the pressure on people to take off on a wave was very intense.

The stakes were getting higher, also. Two other cameras had set up on the Point near to Claire. Success meant you'd probably get your picture in a surf mag. Failure, with a building swell and jagged rocks below... Well, you'd probably get a ride to A&E.

Ezra had experience in this sort of crowd. In a contest he might worry, but freesurfing he tended not to care about getting pushed deep. Lots of surfers were being forced into waves steeper and further behind the rocks than they felt was safe. With so much barging, that seemed the only way to get one.

Ianto understood, though, and he kept to his own game. He knew which waves were best, and how to wait for them. Just like other days, he was having his pick of the biggest, longest and cleanest ones.

He and Ezra were paddling back out, side-by-side, when Ianto explained what he thought: 'There's people in here who surf good but don't properly know the wave,' he told Ezra. 'They're taking off really deep and too shallow. That's because they don't realise how dangerous that ledge section of water is. If you sit outside them, when a proper one comes through they won't be able to swing around in time.'

'Got it,' said Ezra.

'And if you're lucky you might end up pushing them too deep without even trying.'

'Okay.'

Ezra had seen the top locals work this plan before. It helped his own position for that to happen. Ianto was right, and knew the potential risks of a big drop over that wave ledge. He had seen the blood and gore such a mistake could lead to.

Meanwhile, a slight offshore breeze had begun to blow. Again, this was something that never happened on a warm Spring day. Claire, standing on the rocks, knew exactly what Ianto was saying to Ezra. She didn't need to read his lips. Her own experience told her the details.

'Check the wind swinging, Ez! Even the bigger waves are gonna be hollow soon.'

The other two cameras to arrive on the Point were further up than Claire. One was Tim Parfitt, who shot sports all over Wales, including rugby and football. The other was a now-famous local face, Tony John, whose front-page images of the pier getting smashed had made the town famous in the national papers.

'How's the pier looking, Tony?' Claire asked.

'Pretty normal!' he shouted back. 'Nothing we haven't seen plenty of times this year. Spotted waves bending over towards the Point! Soon as I saw the whitewater I had to head over. Getting any?'

'Yeah, some good ones of Ianto,' she shouted.

Their conversation was cut off as Amy Murphy started paddling for a wave. It went steep and dark on her immediately, and as Amy went into the freefall, Claire started pressing. Click... Click-click-click. Watching it through the lens was the only way not to be afraid of the danger Amy was in. As soon as Amy got to the bottom of the wave it lined up and doubled in size. Claire could see water running off the reef in front, and as Amy turned, her board sank below sea-level.

The Point had taken another shift towards deadly. Amy raced out of danger, for now, and Claire let out a quiet, 'Whooop!'

'Get that one?' Tony shouted.

'Not sure,' said Claire. 'You?'

'Nope. I'm too far up. Gonna move now. Hang on, mind if I set up nearer?'

'Be my guest.'

Ezra was at the top of the Point now, after Ianto had gone on the next wave. There was an even bigger one lining up, and Claire shouted to Tony.

'Tony! Look! Stay where you are!'

Tony swung around and aimed his lens at the wave. For some reason that Claire couldn't understand, Ezra drifted over the top without even looking at it.

He's passing it up?

It made no sense. Or did he know something she didn't?

26

'George Schofield, one of Ezra's best friends, took the wave just before it,' Claire remembers. 'At the time, I thought Ezra was mad for not taking that one. He had position. Everyone else was miles out of place. He had worked his way through the line-up perfectly.'

What Claire admires most is how, having got into that right place, Ezra actually waited out one wave. If he hadn't, who knows what would have happened next?

'George didn't get anywhere on his,' she says. 'There was so much jockeying for position that he had to go really late and right under the lip. It was a huge take-off, the heaviest all day. He's one of the best surfers in Britain, George, and he had to use every bit of his skill just to survive the drop.'

Ezra, behind that wave, could hear the rest of the crowd hooting and screaming as George took flight. It was a genuine 'air drop', all the way to the shallow bottom. George surprised himself that he got there in one piece, and didn't seem to mind when the rest of the wave raced away from him. He waited for the explosion to finish, then stepped off and made himself light. Would he hit the rocks?

It was a battering, but George got through the broken wave, and popped up the other side with nothing but a freezing head. Just in time to realise what was in front of him.

Out back, all alone, Ezra had spotted the wave a hundred yards off.

'You could see how determined he was, right away,' recalls Ianto.

Ezra, meanwhile, remembers the slow, patient process of getting into that position: 'I put myself in a part of the line-up where I was comfortable, and just held my ground from there,' he says. He'd waited for this moment and now here it was. *His* wave. He had earned it.

'There's always someone elsc who tries to paddle too, to try to back you up on it, like, as if you're not gonna do it. But this time I was the only one. I think they all realised how much I wanted it.'

In front of the whole arena, a wave had appeared which seemed to have found an angle of its own. As big as anything to have come through that day, it was going to break easier than the others. The thickness in its shape showed it hadn't slowed down properly either. Ezra was the only person with any chance of getting into it early enough. Five yards deeper than anyone else, behind the sharpest rocks on the Point, he spun around, paddled and whispered to himself aloud:

'I'm going. No holding back. Balls to the wall!'

It sounds funny, he'll admit, but this was something he believed helped him on the most challenging waves. And he wasn't done yet. 'I'm Kelly Slater,' he told himself, just quietly enough. 'I'm on the *tour* and I *can* barrel ride. I do this stuff on a *daily basis*.'

It was a superb piece of mind control. It worked. He stroked into the take-off spot with perfect timing, pushed over the top, popped to his feet, looked ahead...

...And then the wave bottomed out.

'As it curled, you could see the barrel would stay open

this time,' says Claire, who had no time to think of anything else.

Ezra's eyes were focussed on where he needed to go, which first of all was downward. By the time he saw the lip-line, he had begun looking up, though. He had a firm hold of his outside rail, and felt his fins catch the water below. So far, so good. As the bottom dropped away, the top half of the wave was still building. This *thing* was dragging water from all around, and preparing to pour itself over the shallow rocks.

By the time Ezra had fixed his line, the lip was over his head. He saw daylight shining through the roof and the water was lit up around him like gold. Sound vanished, and time slowed. The water under him got thinner, as the wave started to twist.

Looking out of the tube, he could see other surfers peering in. One tried to paddle in case Ezra didn't reach them, but then gave up as the wave thickened even more. One moment drifted into another. Noise came back, but it was a new noise. Water echoing against water. He could feel the pressure of air caught in the wave. He was sitting on the pulse. Energy from thousands of miles away, Code Black fury, was running through his veins as the gold light began to fade.

'I did think I *might* make it,' he recalls, the biggest grin ever spreading across his face. 'But then that lip carried on getting further and further away. So I just held on for dear life and tried to make things last as long as possible.'

'How long?'

'Ages. I dunno. Time stopped.'

The foam ball was what pulled him down. His board lifted from beneath him, shook and then began to slide sideways. Darkness came, followed by a gentle dragging of churned water.

What Claire remembers above anything else, though, was the violence that lay just outside that peaceful place. As Ezra was coaxed down and through the vortex, Claire's attention was on the size of the bounce. In front of the wave, everything had exploded skywards.

'The whitewater was bigger than the wave itself,' Claire remembers. 'It blew up behind. I've never seen anything like that. He popped up behind as if nothing had happened though. That was impressive, too. The way Ez reacted to what had just occurred. He didn't celebrate it, or look over to me. Nothing of the sort. He just dusted himself off and began paddling back out there.'

Behind the turbulence and splashing rocks as the wave ran aground, what Claire couldn't see was Ezra's face.

'A grin from ear to ear!' says Ezra. 'Like this! Look!' Just thinking about it can make him take on that same smile, any time, any place.

'Everything that happened after that didn't seem important,' says Claire, and Ezra agrees:

'I don't remember exactly,' he says. 'Well, I surfed for a while longer. I must have done. I tried to get another probably, didn't I? But it was getting too high all of a sudden and was over for the day.'

Claire's theory is that the tide came in a bit extra during that one wave. She thinks Ezra was riding a wave *and* a surge of tide, together. What does he make of the idea?

'Must have,' he says after thinking for a moment. 'That was the end, really. Yeah. After that we all just kind of... Well, rode the swell out. It sort of... went to sleep, slowly. I was so hyped up after that one. I can't really remember much more. Hopefully there will be more like it again next winter.'

27

The ocean's last push? For Claire there was still something very important to worry about.

'Tony! Did you get it? I was out of focus! *Please* say you got that!'

Tony's eyes told her the answer she dreaded. He was too far up the Point. He had been walking as the waves arrived, and wasn't ready. That's the life of a photographer. Tony laughs about it today, and says this was a wave Mother Nature had decided to give to him as a treat. A treat, as in he got to see it with his eyes only, for once.

'Tim! Tim! TIM!' But the other photographer had been on the move, too. He'd shot it, but from an angle that would only show empty wave. Ezra had been in so deep you could only see him from directly in front.

'That was it,' says Claire. 'I thought we would all have to make do with an empty picture of that wave. I laughed. It seemed fitting in a way. The heaviest tube ever caught at the Point, and the only photo taken leaves out the rider!'

She had the wrong shutter speed. That was her excuse. Or was it the motor? She fired too many shots in one go. Ten frames per second! What was she thinking? She had watched through the eyepiece, and Ezra was a blur as he dropped in. The camera had too much stuff in front of it. Too many layers to the image. A piece of water bounced in front! That's what it was. Lying in the back as Steve drove, she was *certain* there was no shot.

Claire never looks at the screen on her camera. It's bad form. It's only when she transfers the files that she sees them for the first time.

She waited two days. The pain had to come and go first. All that balancing on rocks, all that excitement. Her back grew stiff, and she was overcome with agony. The whole time, though, the memory of what she'd seen kept her going.

The memory, and the chance to look at the pictures.

When the time came to download them, she sat nervously in front of the computer. As the transfer counted down, she chatted to Steve. She was so sure the shots of that wave hadn't come out she needed as much distraction as she could get.

'Steve, what was it like being out there?' she asked. 'I *really* want to know.'

His answer might help her forget how she had blown her moment.

'It was just enjoyable,' he said, softly, smiling his usual smile. 'That's the only word. I was stoked just sitting a little inside, and seeing into those tubes. We were close, all of us, seeing it from that angle, in the water. Tubes like that. It must have been pretty much as good as being in them.'

'I enjoyed it, too,' she said. 'That's got to be enough, hasn't it?'

'Of course.'

The transfer was complete, and the file opened up. Claire worked methodically, letting Steve push the 'next' button for her. Ianto's early waves, Rob's tube, George's floater. Then came some shots of Coney, and a portrait of Tony John, thumbs up. Not long later the moment began

83

to appear. Amy's wave, Ianto, George and then Ezra.

She was right. It was a blur. Though you could make out what was happening. It would count as *evidence* that the wave had happened, but flicking through the frames was a frustrating process.

Out of focus.

Out of focus.

Bit better.

Worse! He was in the tube now.

Out of focus.

Bit better.

Worse again…

And then, 'Steve! Wait. Go back!'

<u>28</u>

'I feel privileged to have been able to take it,' says Claire. 'I uploaded it straight away. Weeks later people were still "liking" the shot. Months later, even.'

Ezra had been trying not to think about it at all, meanwhile. He knew how silly it would be to come out of a once-in-a-lifetime session and only think about photos. In a way, he half wished the photographers hadn't been there. It was almost a relief to hear Claire thought it would be out of focus. It meant he didn't need to think about anything but the memory.

Either that, or it was an excuse to hope for another wave like it, some time in the future.

When he found out that there was a good picture after all, he had hardly anything to say. What *could* he say?

'I was just stoked that we'd shown the country what waves can get like round here,' he said. 'Anyone could have got that tube.'

His voice says the right things. A diplomat. "Young surfer catches wave of the decade, stays humble." What other choice did he have?

His face though... His face! That gives it all away. He takes a peek at the image as if he doesn't really want to, and then... There comes the grin.

'Okay, yeah, it's me. Is that what you want? Yeah, okay. I can remember it now. It'll never go away. I don't need the picture anyway.'

Then the grin stretches just that bit further and he adds, 'It helps though! It definitely helps. Thanks Claire!'

For others, this is an image that tells a bigger story, too.

'I've been surfing there nearly thirty-five years,' says Ianto. 'Rarely have I seen waves like that. And if I have I can't really be sure, coz it would have been on rainy days or early in the morning or some time when I was too busy trying to catch them to really remember. Having a picture like that of the waves in our town? Well, it's something to get excited about for all of us, isn't it. That's *our* home break! It's not a bad wave on its day, eh?'

It's *Claire's* image, though. Claire's story, and it's fitting that she has the closing word:

'Once in ten years? Once in thirty-five? Maybe,' she says. 'The thing is, with the ocean, it'll always surprise you again. It's been around longer than any of us. When we're gone, it'll still be here. And anyway, how d'you think the Point got there in the first place? How does sand get made from hard rock? There's power out there. We need reminders of that. Our coast has seen those conditions before. It'll see them again.'

She smiles, and then adds, 'And if that happens to be outside of our lifetimes? Well, what a lovely thought. I take great comfort from that, don't you? All of us, our lives, we're just one wave in a set. I love to be reminded how none of us really matter that much. It's the most important lesson.'

Some waves, though, can live in the memory longer than others.

That's why the surfers keep going.

'Roll on winter,' says Ezra.

Glossary of surf terms used in *Code Black*

- **Beach break**: An area where waves that are good enough to surf break just off a beach, or on a sandbar farther out
- **Bomb**: An exceptionally large set wave
- **Cutback**: A turn cutting back toward the breaking part of the wave
- **Drop in**: Dropping into (engaging) the wave, most often as part of standing up
- **Face**: The forward-facing surface of a breaking wave
- **Fin or Fins**: Fin-shaped inserts on the underside of the back of the board that enable the board to be steered
- **Fins out**: A sharp turn where the surfboard's fins slide off the top of the wave
- **Flat**: No waves
- **Floater**: Riding up on the top of the breaking part of the wave, and coming down with it
- **Getting barrelled**: Riding inside the hollow curl of a wave (sometimes called tube riding)
- **Kook**: A surfer of limited skill
- **Leash**: A cord that is attached to the back of the board, the other end of which wraps around the surfer's ankle
- **Line-up**: The area where most of the waves are starting to break and where most surfers are positioned in order to catch a wave
- **Outside**: The part of the water's surface that is farther from the shore than the area where most waves are breaking
- **Point break**: Area where an underwater rocky point creates waves that are suitable for surfing
- **Set waves**: A group of waves of larger size within a swell
- **Snap**: A quick, sharp turn off the top of a wave
- **Stoked**: Happy, excited

- **Swell**: A series of waves that have traveled from their source in a distant storm, and that will start to break once the swell reaches shallow enough water
- **Tail**: The back end of the board
- **Take-off**: The start of a ride
- **Wax**: Specially formulated surf wax that is applied to upper surface of the board to increase the traction so the surfer's feet do not slip off of the board
- **Whitewater**: As a wave breaks, it continues on as a ridge of turbulence and foam called whitewater
- **Wipeout**: Falling off, or being knocked off, the surfboard when riding a wave

Quick Reads 2015

Code Black: Winter of Storm Surfing – Tom Anderson
Cwtch Me if You Can – Beth Reekles

Quick Reads 2015

My Sporting Heroes – Jason Mohammad
Captain Courage – Gareth Thomas

For more information about **Quick Reads**

and other **Accent Press** titles

please visit

www.accentpress.co.uk

STJV 2/20